Exploration
in the
Renaissance

LYNNE ELLIOTT

 Crabtree Publishing Company
www.crabtreebooks.com

Renaissance World

Author: Lynne Elliott
Editor-in-Chief: Lionel Bender
Editors: Lynn Peppas, Simon Adams, Lizann Flatt
Proofreader: Crystal Sikkens
Project coordinator: Robert Walker
Photo research: Susannah Jayes
Design concept: Robert MacGregor
Designer: Malcolm Smythe
Production coordinator: Margaret Amy Salter
Production: Kim Richardson
Prepress technician: Margaret Amy Salter

With thanks to First Folio.

Cover photo: The Departure of Christopher Columbus from the Port of Palos, Spain.

Photo on page 1: The Pilgrim Fathers arrive in North America.

This book was produced for Crabtree Publishing Company by Bender Richardson White.

Photographs and reproductions:
The Art Archive: page Bibliotheque Nationale, Paris: page 4; Laurie Platt Winfrey: page 7; Musee de la Renaissance (Chateau) Ecouen/ Gianni Dagli Orti: page 10; Private Collection/ Marc Charmet: page 11; Harper Collins Publishers: page 12; Marine Museum, Lisbon/Gianni Dagli Orti: page 16; Museum of the City of New York/ 29.100.709: page 25
Giraudon/Art Resource, NY: cover
The Bridgeman Art Library: Palace of Westminster, London, UK: page 9
The Granger Collection: pages 8, 13, 17
iStockphoto.com: pages 5, 6, 15, 18, 23
Northwind Picture Archives: pages 26, 27, 28, 30, 31
Topfoto: pages 19, 20; The British Library/ HIP: page 14; The Image Works: pages 21, 22; Print Collector/HIP: pages 1, 24, 29

Library and Archives Canada Cataloguing in Publication

Elliott, Lynne, 1968-
    Exploration in the Renaissance / Lynne Elliott.

(Renaissance world)
Includes index.
ISBN 978-0-7787-4593-8 (bound).--ISBN 978-0-7787-4613-3 (pbk.)

    1. Discoveries in geography--European--Juvenile literature.
2. Renaissance--Juvenile literature. 3. America--Discovery and exploration--Juvenile literature. I. Title. II. Series: Renaissance world (St. Catharines, Ont.)

G175.E45 2009   j910.9'024   C2008-907901-9

Library of Congress Cataloging-in-Publication Data

Elliott, Lynne, 1968-
    Exploration in the Renaissance / Lynne Elliott.
        p. cm. -- (Renaissance world)
    Includes index.
    ISBN 978-0-7787-4613-3 (pbk. : alk. paper) -- ISBN 978-0-7787-4593-8 (reinforced library binding : alk. paper)
    1. Discoveries in geography--European--Juvenile literature. 2. Renaissance--Juvenile literature. 3. America--Discovery and exploration--Juvenile literature. I. Title. II. Series.

G175.E55 2009
910.9'024--dc22

2008052601

Crabtree Publishing Company

www.crabtreebooks.com   1-800-387-7650

Published in Canada
Crabtree Publishing
616 Welland Ave.
St. Catharines, Ontario
L2M 5V6

Published in the United States
Crabtree Publishing
PMB16A
350 Fifth Ave., Suite 3308
New York, NY 10118

Published in the United Kingdom
Crabtree Publishing
White Cross Mills
High Town, Lancaster
LA1 4XS

Published in Australia
Crabtree Publishing
386 Mt. Alexander Rd.
Ascot Vale (Melbourne)
VIC 3032

Contents

The Roots of Exploration

The Age of Exploration was a period from the 1400s to the 1600s during which Europeans sailed around the world looking for sea routes to Asia and India. On their journeys they discovered lands and people they never knew existed.

The Renaissance

The Age of Exploration took place during the European Renaissance, which lasted from about 1300 to 1600. It was a time of great cultural achievement, when scholars and artists were interested in ancient Greek and Roman ideas in art, literature, government, and science. It was also a time when people were filled with a spirit of adventure and had a genuine curiosity about the world.

Renaissance Advancements

In the time immediately before the Renaissance, Medieval times or the Middle Ages, Europeans knew little about the world beyond their shores. Only a few had ever traveled afar. Medieval Europeans did not have the tools, such as accurate maps, to navigate across great seas.

During the Renaissance, scientists rediscovered ancient books about astronomy, geography, and cartography, or mapmaking, that helped them gather geographical knowledge about their world. They improved **celestial navigation** by adopting **pre-existing** aids, such as the compass and astrolabe, to help them sail across uncharted oceans.

Renaissance shipbuilders, particularly those in Portugal, designed sturdy, seaworthy ships known as caravels, with new rigs of masts and sails, that could sail across open oceans.

Traders carried luxury goods over thousands of miles on camel and horse caravans from Asia to Middle Eastern ports. From there they were brought to European coastal towns on Italian ships.

TIMELINE

1416: Prince Henry begins encouraging exploration of West Africa

1487–88: Bartolomeu Dias is the first to sail around Africa's Cape of Good Hope

1492: Christopher Columbus reaches the Bahamas

1494: Treaty of Tordesillas divides the New World between Spain and Portugal

1498: Vasco da Gama becomes the first European to sail from Europe to India

1519–22: Ferdinand Magellan's crew **circumnavigates** the globe

1519–21: Hernán Cortés leads the Spanish conquest of the Aztec empire in Mexico

1607: First permanent English colony in America

1607: Henry Hudson first hired to find a northern sea passage to the Indies

From Trade to Exploration

One of the earliest motives for Renaissance exploration was the search for a sea route to the spice-rich areas of India and Asia. During the 1100s and 1200s, Europeans began to import more and more luxury goods from the East. Turkish and Arabian traders imposed high taxes and toll prices onto the goods. By the time the items reached Europe, they could cost hundreds of times more than the original price. European rulers and merchants wanted to find a way to trade directly with the East without Arabian and Turkish interference. Since the Arabs kept their trade routes a secret, the Europeans looked for eastern trade routes by way of the world's great oceans.

The Goods

Europeans used saffron, ginger, cloves, cinnamon, and pepper to flavor their food and to make medicine and cosmetics. Fabrics, such as Chinese silk and Egyptian and Indian cotton, were imported and colored with dyes made from Eastern plants, such as indigo and henna. African ivory and semi-precious stones were made into jewelry, while gold and silver were minted into coins.

The astrolabe helped Renaissance explorers find their way across the oceans by using the position of stars or the Sun in the sky to tell them where they were.

The Age of Exploration

Advances in shipbuilding and navigation had made it possible to explore farther than before. Renaissance explorers, monarchs, and merchants wanted to expand their personal wealth and power and spread Christianity throughout the world.

Map from a Spanish atlas of the Molucca Islands in Indonesia. The islands were called the Spice Islands because of the many different spices that grew there in the wild.

New Wealth

Explorers, rulers, and merchants knew that there were enormous profits to be made by bringing luxury goods, such as spices and silks, to Europe from the East. The voyages to Africa, and later to the Americas, were also searches for gold. Europeans used gold as currency, or money. Gold could be brought back to Europe, minted into coins, and deposited into royal treasuries.

Political Power

Medieval monarchs were too busy securing power in their own lands to search out trading routes and overseas territories. Renaissance monarchs, however, reduced the power of the nobility within their kingdoms. With fewer internal troubles, they were more willing to look outward and expand their kingdoms by dominating different lands and peoples around the world. The larger the geographic **empire** a ruler had, the more political power they held.

Religion

Together with the church, European rulers wanted to spread Christianity to non-Christian people of Asia, Africa, and America. Christian monarchs, such as Isabella of Spain, sent Catholic **missionaries** on voyages to **convert** indigenous, or native, people to Christianity. She believed this was her duty to God. Prince Henry of Portugal wanted to defeat **Muslim** rulers in Africa and convert the people to Christianity.

Competition

The race to find a sea route to the East started with the Portuguese and the Spanish. By the late 1500s, other European countries saw the huge profits that the Portuguese and the Spanish were making from exploration. Monarchs and merchants from England, France, and the Netherlands began to sponsor their own voyages of exploration. Their ships sailed in the northern part of the Atlantic Ocean, looking for a sea route to Asia, which led to the discovery, exploration, and colonization of North America.

Merchant Companies

In the late 1500s and 1600s, merchants formed companies that asked monarchs for charters, or written permission, to fund explorations to new lands in the hope of finding new trade items to bring back to Europe. Monarchs granted these companies a monopoly, or sole rights to trade, in the area they explored. In return, the companies gave the monarch a percentage of the profits and claimed the new land for the monarch.

In 1492, King Ferdinand of Spain expelled the Muslim Moors from the south of the country. He created a unified Spain which allowed him to look for other parts of the world to rule.

Organizing a Voyage

A lot of planning went into a voyage of exploration. An explorer had to get royal approval, funding, ships, supplies, and a crew. Only when these items were secured, could the dangerous and difficult voyage begin.

Explorers

Some explorers were from the merchant class of Renaissance society. They grew up near important shipping ports. They signed on with merchant ships, where they received their training in sailing and navigation. Other Renaissance explorers were noblemen and soldiers. Instead of sailing experience, they had the leadership abilities to organize and command a voyage. Despite the different social classes explorers came from, they were all curious, brave, and sought fame and fortune.

A German woodcut, 1486, showing the building of a ship, the most expensive item in a voyage. Explorers often needed three or more ships. One was used only for supplies, but a third, extra ship was useful in case one was destroyed by a storm or in a battle.

Finding Funding

Explorers could not afford to pay for a voyage by themselves. They had to raise money for the ships, crews' salaries, and supplies. They usually approached monarchs, wealthy nobles, merchant companies, or business people and convinced them to finance their journey. The major sponsor of the voyage usually supplied the ships. In return, the explorer would claim new lands for the monarch and new trade routes for the merchant company.

Gathering Supplies

Ships were equipped with weapons such as cannons, gunpowder, crossbows, suits of armor, and swords needed to capture trading towns or to fight pirates at sea. Explorers tried to carry enough food, water, and wine to last the voyage, as well as wood for cooking fires and repairs. Ships also carried trade goods, which included mirrors, glass beads, bolts of fabric, and bells. Later voyagers carried metal cooking utensils and metal fishhooks to trade.

Recruiting a Crew

In town squares and by the waterfront, where unemployed men usually gathered, **criers** announced the need for a crew and the benefits of signing up. A crew needed to include pages, or ships' boys, who were servants, inexperienced sailors called apprentices, and experienced mariners.

A number of specialists were needed to keep the ship in good repair. Coopers made and repaired barrels that held most of the supplies including food, water, and wine. Caulkers sealed the seams in wooden boats to make them waterproof. Carpenters, sail makers, and blacksmiths repaired damage to a ship's wooden hull, sails, and rigging. Professional soldiers and gunners defended the ships against attacks by other traders,

Different Duties

An explorer usually acted as the commanding officer. Captains serving underneath him oversaw each ship in the fleet. A captain's assistant, the master, made decisions about sailing the ship and managing the crew. The pilot, or navigator, assisted the master by charting the ship's direction and location at sea. Marshals maintained the crew's discipline and gave out punishments.

enemy countries, and indigenous peoples. An explorer might recruit a doctor, surgeon, or pharmacist, called an apothecary, to take care of the crew's health. Missionaries and priests traveled on board in order to reach the non-Christian peoples in other lands.

Explorer John Cabot receives a charter from King Henry VII of England. An explorer would secure a charter, or an agreement, for himself outlining what titles and authority, rights over trade, and share of profits would be given to him as the leader of a successful voyage of discovery.

Life On Board a Ship

Living on board a ship was not easy. Ships were small and their voyages lasted for months. Sailors worked hard, lived in cramped conditions, and did not have much fresh food or clean water.

Living Conditions

Space was given to supplies and cargo, not to the crew. Most sailors slept on deck, where they tied themselves down to prevent them from falling overboard. They were often splashed by the waves. In bad weather, they might have slept below deck on the cargo. The captain and important officers might have slept in a bunk or cabin below deck.

Some ships had bathrooms, or simple toilets that were open-bottom boxes that hung over the side of a ship and were washed out by seawater. Sailors would wash in calm seas, or not wash at all. They did not risk shaving on a rocking ship, so they usually had beards by the end of the journey.

Food and Water

Sailors ate preserved foods, such as salted beef, pork, or fish, dried foods, such as oatmeal, rice, beans, almonds, and hard biscuits made from flour and salt. They flavored their food with garlic, which kept well. They also ate dried fruit such as raisins and fruit in jams. Sailors had a daily ration of drink, usually wine, water, or ale.

On deck during good weather the crew took turns cooking their hot meals in large pots heated over a cook-box, a hooded box with a sand bed. In bad weather, they ate food that didn't need to be cooked. If food ran short, crews ate moldy and bug-infested biscuits, leather, and sawdust. They also cooked shipboard rats and drank smelly water.

A model of a flagship. The flagship was the one the commanding officer, usually the explorer, sailed in. It flew his personal flag.

Passing Time

Sailors told stories, played practical jokes on each other, or listened to a crewmember sing or play an instrument. They sometimes carved scrap pieces of wood and bone and practiced tying nautical knots on the many lengths of rope lying around the deck. They also played games, such as cards and dice. When the sea was calm, they went swimming or fished with lines and hooks, providing a welcome addition to their diets.

The crew also had daily prayers that were sung several times a day, or Mass if there was a priest on board. These services were important because they prayed for the sailors' protection at sea.

Shipboard Etiquette

Crew behavior was guided by a set of rules. They were to avoid using bad language that might offend God, who protected their ship. They could play cards but not bet on the outcome, since it led to other sailors' poverty, ill-feelings between winners and losers, and fighting. They had to obey their superior officers. In return, officers had to treat the crew with some respect, such as only hitting them once while reprimanding them.

Stopping at a trading post, like this one in the West Indies in 1565, would be a brief but welcome change to life on board a ship.

Hard Work

Days and nights were filled with the work of adjusting the sails and rigging, repairing leaks, mending ripped sails and frayed ropes, pumping out water from the bottom of the ship, keeping the deck clean and clear, cooking food, and watching for land or enemy ships. The crew worked in shifts, called watches, which alternated every four hours as timed by a thirty-minute sand clock, which was turned by a boy servant.

Dangers of Exploration

As if life on board wasn't difficult enough, Renaissance sailors had to contend with many dangers while on a voyage. Storms, diseases, and violence threatened the lives of many crew members, while some feared the unknown.

Shipwrecks and Sinking

Shipwrecks and sinking were a constant danger for sailors. Crashing waves or errors in navigation caused ships to run aground or to smash into rocks, splintering and sinking the ship. Ships sailing in icy waters were hit and sunk by icebergs or ice floes. Sailors fell overboard and drowned during bad weather and storms, including hurricanes, which ripped the ships apart and sent them to the bottom of the ocean.

Sickness

Sailors got sick, often from malnutrition caused by a lack of fresh food for months at a time. Sailors suffered dysentery, a severe diarrhea caused by rotten food and dirty water. They also got scurvy, a bleeding disease brought on by a diet lacking the Vitamin C found in fresh fruit and vegetables. Diseases, such as influenza, measles, and smallpox, spread easily from one person to another in a ship's cramped conditions. Sailors also died from infections to wounds caused by shipboard accidents or by fighting in battles.

Explorers faced the real danger of being shipwrecked, as shown here in this painting of Dutch ships tossed in a storm and smashing into a rocky coast.

This woodcut from 1550 shows the sea monsters that were thought to live in the North Atlantic as well as the animals found in northern lands.

Piracy

Ships were in danger of being robbed at sea. Pirates would attack ships for their cargo or raid coastal towns for their riches. Pirates operated wherever there were **commercial** ships and trading activity. They were considered outlaws in every country of the world. During the Renaissance, however, there arose a type of raider called a privateer who, unlike a pirate, was given a license by their European monarch to capture and steal cargo from other countries' ships.

Land and Sea Battles

Renaissance sailors were also expected to be soldiers. Portuguese sailors lost their lives fighting against Arab warships sent to destroy Portuguese trading ships in the Indian Ocean. Sailors were also killed or injured while fighting indigenous people for control of the land, such as when Spanish sailors fought the indigenous populations in the Caribbean, Mexico, Central and South America, and the Philippines.

Secrets and Treachery

There was a lot of jealousy between countries over who would explore successful trade routes to the East. Famous explorers, especially the early Portuguese, kept their journeys secret for fear of their lives. They hid the daily records of their expedition, which were written in a ship's logbooks, so they would not be found or stolen by enemy spies. Even before their voyages, explorers were in danger of being poisoned or murdered by agents of monarchs afraid of sharing trade routes with other countries. Explorers often hired bodyguards for their own personal protection.

Maps and Navigation

Renaissance explorers ventured far beyond the coastlines of Europe into the open oceans. Without land in sight, they needed to determine their ship's exact position and direction at sea. Advances in mapmaking and navigation during this period made this possible.

Renaissance Maps

During the 1400s, portolan charts replaced religious maps, which had placed the holy city of Jerusalem at the center of the world, surrounded by only three continents: Asia, Africa, and Europe. Mapmakers began to add horizontal lines, or lines of latitude, onto the portolan charts. These lines were labeled with numbers, called degrees, which indicated distance north and south from the equator. Later Renaissance mapmakers added vertical lines to maps in order to measure longitude, the distance east or west a ship had traveled.

Portolan charts showed the seaports and harbors along Europe's coastline. They used a series of lines, called rhumb lines, that criss-crossed the chart to indicate sea routes to coastal ports. This map of Europe from 1570 has lines of latitude but no lines of longitude.

Picturing the World

Many voyages had chartmakers on board who sketched maps of coastlines, harbors, islands, and rivers of recently discovered lands. When this information was brought back to Europe, mapmakers added it to their existing maps. The first globe, made by German mapmaker Martin Behaim, was constructed in 1492, just before Columbus's voyage to the New World. It had over 1,000 place names and included legends, merchandise, and trade routes of the then known world.

Tools to Determine Latitude

To determine their latitude, navigators measured the height of the Sun or stars in the sky. For example, the closer they were to the equator, the lower the North Star appeared in the sky. The astrolabe, a round wooden or brass instrument, used two plates on a rotating arm to measure the angle between the zenith, or point directly overhead, and the Sun or a star. From that, navigators determined their latitude. It was difficult to line up the celestial objects in the sight on a rolling ship, and could result in errors of over 300 miles (480 km).

The cross-staff, a cross-shaped, wooden instrument, determined the distance of the Sun or the North Star down to the horizon. A navigator put one end called the main staff just below his eye and slid the crosspiece down until the top end lined up with the Sun or star and the bottom end lined up with the horizon. Markings on the main staff, where it met the crosspiece, indicated the degree of latitude.

The quadrant, shaped like a slice of pie, has a plumb-line hanging from its top point. When lined up with a star or the Sun, the point at which the plumb-line crossed the curved edge at the bottom indicated the object's height in degrees.

Determining Longitude

Longitude was determined by dead reckoning, an estimate of the distance the ship had traveled. To measure distance, the ship's speed was multiplied with the amount of time it had been traveling. To measure speed, sailors threw a rope overboard. A piece of wood tied to the end carried the rope away from the moving ship. The rope had knots tied at intervals usually around 47 feet (14 m). Sailors counted the number of knots that were released in 30 seconds, as measured by a 30-second sand glass. Measuring this way was inaccurate because speed changed due to currents and winds.

A magnetic needle on a compass face always points north, so from that a navigator could determine which direction his ship was sailing in. Introduced to European sailors by the Arabs, it was one of the most valuable instruments for Renaissance explorers.

Early Portuguese Explorations

In the 1400s, the Portuguese began to explore the west coast of Africa in search of riches to trade. Each voyage sailed farther south into uncharted waters and stimulated more voyages that eventually found the sea route around Africa to the trade-rich Indies.

Exploring West Africa

Lured by rumors of gold and a desire to conquer Muslims in Africa, Prince Henry of Portugal began financing yearly expeditions down the coast of Western Africa. The voyages Henry sponsored dispelled myths about monsters and storms in the "Sea of Darkness," as the Atlantic Ocean was called. They also brought back information on winds, currents, landmarks, geography, and observations about the stars.

All of this knowledge allowed Portuguese sailors to push farther and farther south down the African coastline and trade copper, horses, cloth, and other goods for gold, ivory, and other precious goods from the Guinea coast of West Africa. This African trade brought great wealth back to Portugal and helped to provide funds for even more expeditions.

Prince Henry of Portugal (1394–1460) with his cartographers and captains. He was known as Henry the Navigator because of his interest in exploration. He financed many voyages. Not since ancient times had European ships sailed south of the equator.

African Slave Trade

Henry allowed his sailors to bring African captives back to Europe. At first they were to be questioned about the geography, people, trading routes, and activities in their homeland. By 1444, expeditions were being made solely for bringing Africans back to Portugal as slaves. It is estimated that every year 1,000 slaves were brought to Portugal to be sold throughout Europe. This slave trade soon evolved into the trans-Atlantic slave trade that brought misery and death to millions of Africans for the next 300 years, until the widespread **abolition** of the slave trade and slavery in the 1800s.

Rounding The Cape

After Prince Henry's death, the monarchy continued to encourage exploration, aiming to find a sea route to India, the land of spices and precious gems. In 1487, King John II of Portugal financed Portuguese navigator Bartolomeu Dias and a fleet of three ships to sail farther down the coast than anyone had

Caravels

The Portuguese led the Age of Exploration because of their advances in ship design. They designed the caravel, which was a slim, light, and fast wooden vessel. Caravels usually carried a crew of 20 and had a lot of cargo space for trading goods. They had lateen, or triangular, sails that were used to steer along coastlines, and square sails that were used for speed in open water.

gone before. In spite of fierce storms, low supplies of food and water, and a crew weakened by disease, Dias managed to sail around the southernmost tip of Africa and entered the Indian Ocean in 1488. He failed to reach India because his crew demanded to go home, but Dias's journey verified that the South African coast opened up to the Indian Ocean. It also proved that the Indian Ocean was not surrounded by land as ancient maps indicated, but could be reached by ship.

Detail from an atlas in 1502 showing El Mina, a Portuguese slave-trading fortress on the African coast. Several coastal islands were claimed by Portugal and made into colonies that grew grapes for wine and sugar cane harvested by African slaves.

East to India

In 1497, King Manuel I of Portugal hired navigator Vasco da Gama to sail beyond the point where Dias had turned around. Despite hardships like those Dias had faced, da Gama rounded the Cape of Good Hope into the Indian Ocean. From there he sailed northward up the East Coast of Africa, discovering important Arab trading cities, including Malindi, the largest East African trading port. With the help of an Arab navigator, da Gama's crew sailed east across the Indian Ocean to India, where in 1498, da Gama landed in Calicut, the richest and most important port in southern India.

That voyage gave the Portuguese the sea route to India. It was the first step in Portuguese attempts to forge partnerships with traders in the East, which led to Portugal's control of the spice trade. Eventually, Portugal set up trading colonies that shipped spices, porcelain, wax, paper, and precious jewels back to Portugal's capital, Lisbon, where they were sold to European merchants for huge profits.

Dias called the southernmost tip of Africa the Cape of Storms, because of the violent storms his ships encountered there. Portugal's king renamed it the Cape of Good Hope in order to encourage further exploration.

Reaching China and Japan

The discovery of the sea route to the Indian Ocean opened up trade to the rest of Asia. By 1511, the Portuguese had captured the city of Malacca, in Malaysia, built a fort there, and taken over the rich trade of the Spice Islands. By the 1520s, they had reached traders in Macau on the Chinese coast, and by the 1540s they were trading with the Japanese in Nagasaki. By the early 1600s, the Portuguese lost their dominance over trade in Asia. Powerful Dutch and English trading companies, both called the East India Company, destroyed Portuguese ships and set up their own trading posts.

Circling the Globe

Ferdinand Magellan, denied a request for a voyage by the Portuguese king, offered Spain his idea of finding a western sea route to India. In 1519, with five ships and 270 men, he crossed the Atlantic Ocean and sailed around South America into the Pacific Ocean across to the Philippines. There Magellan was killed in a battle, but the crew continued around Africa and home to Spain in 1522. Magellan's voyage proved that Asia could be reached by sailing west. The crew's navigational information helped confirm the size of Earth.

Larger vessels, called carracks, were sometimes used for long ocean journeys, since they were sturdy in the open ocean and had space for more supplies and sailors than the smaller caravel.

Spain and the New World

Italian explorer Christopher Columbus was convinced that the shortest route to Asia was westward across the Atlantic Ocean. He did not know that a huge landmass lay between Europe and Asia. He never found the route to Asia, but his voyages established lasting contact between Europe and the Americas.

First Encounter

After a two-month sail across the Atlantic Ocean, Columbus's three ships landed on an island in the Bahamas in October 1492. He then sailed from the Bahamas to Cuba and Hispaniola, now known as Haiti and the Dominican Republic, and claimed them all for Spain. Columbus returned to Spain with enough gold masks and ornaments to convince the monarch to sponsor more voyages and establish settlements as trading colonies there. He made three more voyages for Spain to the lands now called Puerto Rico, Jamaica, the Virgin Islands, Trinidad, Venezuela, Panama, and Honduras.

Settlements

On his second voyage, Columbus returned to the Caribbean not as an explorer but as a conqueror. He brought 1,500 sailors, soldiers, missionaries, and male settlers, including craftsmen and farmers, who wanted to clear the land and build houses, churches, and a port for shipping goods back to Europe.

The first Spanish settlements in the New World were on the island of Hispaniola. The first settlement, called La Navidad, was destroyed by native inhabitants. The second settlement, called Isabella after the Spanish queen, was abandoned as settlers moved to Santo Domingo, which became the center of the Spanish colonial administration.

Columbus arrives in the Bahamas in 1492. There he made the first European contact with the native peoples of the Caribbean, the friendly Tainos, or Arawaks, and the unfriendly Caribs.

Native Slavery

With Columbus's permission, the settlers forced native peoples into slavery. Each native had a quota of gold they had to give to the settlers. Refusal was punishable by death. They were also forced to hand over what food they had to the settlers. The Spanish considered the native peoples enemies of war, as they had risen up against early Spanish settlements and killed Spanish settlers.

Missionaries

Columbus's second voyage carried Christian missionaries to the New World to convert the natives. The natives were supposed to receive religious instruction, decide freely to convert to Christianity, and be baptized by the missionaries. Instead, Spanish soldiers read them an **ultimatum**, called the *Requirimiento*, telling them to accept the authority of Spain and the Church or be considered enemies of war and be forced into slavery. The soldiers also wanted the natives to become "more Spanish," and forced them to live in towns where they could observe how the Spanish lived and attend religious services. It didn't take long for the missionaries to complain to the Spanish crown about this form of conversion and the brutal treatment of the natives by the Spanish authorities.

Coming to America

Amerigo Vespucci, an Italian who explored the east coast of South America in two voyages between 1499 and 1502, realized that the landmass he was exploring was not Asia, as Columbus claimed, but a continent previously unknown to Europeans. He called it "The New World" in published letters about his journeys. In 1507, German mapmaker Martin Waldseemuller produced a map including Vespucci's descriptions of the New World, naming the land on the map America, the Latin form of Vespucci's first name.

Natives of the New World meet explorers and missionaries from the Old World. The encounter would forever change many aspects of life for both peoples.

The Conquistadors

Columbus's discovery motivated Spanish soldiers, called conquistadors, to sail to the New World. These men were mostly knights, fighting members of the upper class in Spain, who had no land from which to earn money so they sought fame, titles, and income. Conquistadors overwhelmed the peoples of the Americas to set up colonies in the new lands and ship gold and silver, food, and other trade goods back to Europe.

Conquering Mexico

The Aztec empire was a powerful and wealthy empire that controlled millions of people in Central and Southern Mexico from the 1300s to the 1500s. Its capital, Tenochtitlán, was built on an island in the middle of Lake Texcoco. At the time of the conquest, the city had a population of about 200,000 people. Montezuma II ruled the city and surrounding lands.

Hernán Cortés, a conquistador, led the defeat of the Aztecs with the help of native allies and powerful European weapons, such as guns, steel swords, and heavy warhorses that the Aztecs had never seen before. Yet the largest contributor to the Aztec defeat was probably smallpox, a contagious disease that causes high fevers and skin sores, which killed thousands of natives and weakened their ability to fight off the Spanish.

Spanish soldiers were given land and native people to work it. The Aztecs who survived

Conquistador Vasco Núñez de Balboa, who in 1513 marched across Panama and became the first European to see the Pacific Ocean. Pizarro was his second in command.

were forced to work as slaves, mining for gold and silver and rebuilding Tenochtitlán. The city was rebuilt with Spanish-style buildings and churches replaced temples. The city was renamed Mexico City.

Conquering South America

The Inca empire was the largest empire in South America. It was centered in the Andes mountains of present-day Peru, but included lands in Argentina, Chile, Bolivia, and Ecuador. Its capital was the city of Cuzco, where the ruler, the Sapa Inca, lived and ran his empire of millions of people with the help of family members and a strong military.

After the Aztecs were defeated, their customs and religion, such as their belief in the five creations of the world, as shown on this stone, were replaced by Spanish beliefs.

Ruling the Incas

The Spanish conquistador Francisco Pizarro reached the northern frontier of the empire by ship in 1530. The Inca people had been devastated by disease and had just ended a civil war. In a surprise ambush, Pizarro and his men, with horses and guns, captured the Inca leader and slaughtered 4,000 Inca nobles. Without leaders, the empire fell apart and the Spanish took over the capital in 1533. Pizarro marched through Peru destroying temples, seizing gold and silver, and killing Inca people or forcing them to work as slaves in silver mines or on land given to Spanish settlers.

Pizarro's conquest of the Inca empire allowed Spain to control vast areas of South America, export gold and silver to Europe, and set up a new government capital in Lima. The Inca way of life was totally destroyed and replaced by Spanish customs, language, and the Christian religion.

Fountain of Youth

Juan Ponce de León was the first European to reach Florida. Legend has it that, in addition to new land and gold, he was searching for a magical fountain whose waters could make an old person young again by bathing in it. He never found this fountain of youth but claimed La Florida, Spanish for "the flowered one," for Spain.

The Northwest Passage

Renaissance explorers from England, France, and the Netherlands imagined they could reach Asia by sailing north and westward around the top of the North American landmass, a route known as the Northwest Passage. They failed to find the passage, but the voyages helped these nations stake their claims for territory on the new continent.

English Attempts

The earliest attempts to find a northern sea route to Asia were made by John Cabot, who sailed west from England in 1497 and landed in Newfoundland or Nova Scotia on the east coast of Canada. Cabot thought he was in Asia. Only after Vespucci's voyages did explorers realize that the land was a continent previously unknown to Europeans.

English and Dutch merchant companies sent English explorer Henry Hudson on four voyages starting in 1607. He did not find the Northwest Passage, but found rich whaling areas near the Spitsbergen Islands in the Arctic. Europeans used whale blubber, or fat, in soap or as oil for lamps and grease on wheels. His discovery of the huge bay in northern Canada, now called Hudson's Bay, allowed England to claim the fur trade in that area. In 1670, the English king granted a charter, or exclusive trading rights, over the Hudson's Bay area to a group of merchants known as the Hudson's Bay Company.

John Cabot, exploring on behalf of England, discovers land. His discovery enabled England to claim land and establish settlements in North America.

A map showing the Dutch colony of New Amsterdam, on Manhattan Island in present-day New York City. Dutch settlers purchased the island of Manhattan from a native tribe for $24 in 1626.

Finding the Passage

The Northwest Passage was not found until 1906 when the Norwegian explorer Roald Amundsen navigated the route. The passage is, unfortunately, rarely profitable to use as a shipping route because it is frozen most of the time.

The Dutch Discoveries

In 1609, the Dutch merchant company called the Dutch East India Company hired Henry Hudson to try to find the passage to Asia. Hudson sailed across the Atlantic and explored the east coast of America. He sailed up the Hudson River and allowed the Dutch to claim land in the New World. Dutch families settled the areas around Fort Orange, near what is now Albany, New York, and around the area of New York City, which they called New Amsterdam.

France's Exploration

The French king, Francis I, also wanted to find the Northwest Passage. In 1534, he sent French explorer Jacques Cartier on an expedition. Cartier explored the east coast of Canada and claimed the lands for France by erecting a cross on the Gaspé Peninsula.

On two later expeditions, Cartier explored the St. Lawrence River and tried to set up a settlement at a place called Charlesbourg-Royal. It failed because, due to bad weather and disease, the settlers barely survived the first winter. Still, Cartier's exploration attracted other explorers who settled along the St. Lawrence valley and established the fur trade between France and its new colony.

Fur Trade

During the late Renaissance, hats made from beaver **pelts** became very popular. As a result, beaver was overhunted and nearly became extinct in Europe. As early as Cartier's expeditions, Europeans traded with native trappers for fur pelts and shipped them home. By 1599, France's first trading post, in Tadoussac along the St. Lawrence, shipped thousands of pelts back to France.

Settlements and Colonies

During the Age of Exploration, European nations laid claim to areas around the world. They established colonies, or settlements, in these places. Settlers had many reasons, mainly based on money and religion, for leaving their European homeland and venturing to unknown lands far away.

Spices

As early as 1510, the Portuguese set up a colony in Goa, India, to ship valuable goods, such as spices, back to Europe. The settlers, including merchants, traders, sailors, and government and church officials, erected Portuguese-style mansions, built a marketplace, demolished **Hindu** temples, and built Catholic churches.

Gold

The main goal of Spanish settlement in the Americas was gold. Once gold and silver were discovered in Mexico and South America, settlers began arriving. By 1574, Spanish settlers had established over 200 cities and towns throughout North and South America. These cities included Spanish-style houses, government buildings, libraries, schools, Catholic churches, and even two distinguished universities in Mexico City and Lima, Peru. Many Spaniards also came to the New World to become farmers on estates that grew grain, raised livestock, and produced sugar.

Taking Sides

In 1608, Champlain allied himself with the Huron and Algonquin nations in a raid against their enemies, the Iroquois. From then on the Iroquois, who were fierce warriors, became enemies of the French and **allied** themselves with the British.

Samuel de Champlain made four expeditions to Canada from 1603 to 1615, opening up the region for French settlement and establishing good relations with the Huron and Algonquin.

Jamestown, Virginia was the first permanent English settlement in North America. Settlers suffered from swarms of mosquitoes, shortages of food and fresh water, diseases, malnutrition, and attacks by the local Powhatan people.

Fur

The first French settlers came to North America for beaver fur, a valuable good used to make hats and other items of clothing. In 1608, French explorer Samuel de Champlain founded a fur trading post along the St. Lawrence called Quebec in order to acquire furs from the local Huron natives. From this post, he sent out traders, called *coureurs des bois*, or runners of the woods, to live among the native North Americans in order to trade fur. Despite the early settlers' hardships, including harsh winter weather, lack of food, malnutrition, and death, the settlement of Quebec became the first permanent French settlement in Canada.

Land

Some English settlers came to North America on voyages sponsored by merchant companies. Changes in agriculture during the Renaissance drove many farmers off their lands, and they were willing to leave England for a chance to make a living elsewhere. The companies paid for ships and supplies to set up a trading colony in the hope that settlers would harvest crops and natural resources that could be shipped back for sale in England and Europe. These products included fish, fur, lumber, wheat, rice, and tobacco.

The English merchant company, the Virginia Company, sent a group of settlers to Jamestown, Virginia. Although they were originally sent to find gold, which proved futile, they began to grow tobacco, a crop they had learned about from native North Americans. Tobacco soon became one of the most profitable exports from Virginia.

Religion

Many English settlers came to North America to seek religious freedom. In England, strict Protestants, called Separatists, were harassed by the less strict members of the Protestant Church of England. In 1608, a group of separatists left England and settled in the Netherlands. In 1620, they decided to create their own society in a new land. They gained a grant of land from the English Virginia Company and in 1620, 102 of them sailed across the Atlantic in the *Mayflower*. They landed in Plymouth, near Cape Cod, Massachusetts. These settlers were later referred to as pilgrims, a term used to describe people who travel for religious reasons. The Pilgrim Fathers, as we now call them, were mostly farmers. They arrived just before winter, but the lack of food and supplies, the harsh weather, disease, and starvation, took over half of them in the first year.

The Pilgrims were soon followed by another group of strict Protestants, called Puritans, who were also escaping the Church of England. They settled around Boston and created the Massachusetts Bay colony.

The Pilgrims were helped by members of the local Wampanoag people, who gave them food to get them through the winter. The following fall, in 1621, the Pilgrims celebrated a three-day harvest festival, as was the tradition back in England, to thank the Wampanoag for their help. This day is now celebrated as Thanksgiving Day.

Conversion

Religious conversion of non-Christian peoples also motivated Europeans to travel abroad. Catholic missionaries worked among the Hindu people in India's Portuguese colonies and also with the native peoples in New France and in the Spanish colonies in the Americas and the Philippines. French Protestant missionaries worked among the native Tupi people of Brazil.

The Pilgrim Fathers arrive in North America. They sailed there to escape religious persecution in Europe.

Changing Relationships with Native Peoples

Early contact between the settlers and the native peoples of North America was for the most part friendly. The natives often offered help to struggling settlers. As more settlers arrived and claimed lands that rightly belonged to the natives, they were pushed off their lands and the relationship between the two peoples soured. Previously friendly tribes, such as the Wampanoags, Pequots, and Narragansetts in New England, waged war on the English settlers. The native Americans lost. Many survivors were sold to enemy peoples or sent to the West Indies as slaves to work on sugar plantations.

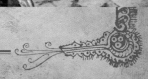

Columbian Exchange

The Columbian Exchange is the name for the exchange of animals, plants, people, diseases, and ideas between Europe and the Americas that followed Columbus's voyages to the New World. The exchange had long-lasting effects for both worlds.

Food and Crops

Foods from the New World, such as potatoes, became a staple in European diets, as did cocoa to make chocolate, tomatoes, and maize, or corn. American crops, such as vanilla, kidney beans, squash, pumpkin, coconuts, pineapples, and chilies, gave the European diet more variety and may have led to better health. In return, settlers brought grains such as wheat and barley from Europe, as well as grapes, oranges, figs, rice, bananas, and olives.

Animals

There were no sheep, cattle, oxen, or swine in the Americas when Columbus arrived. Europeans later brought them over for their meat and milk. These animals reproduced rapidly and grazed upon the vegetation, which probably led to the extinction of certain grasses, roots, and fruits. Since many native North Americans had a vegetarian diet, their food supply was depleted.

Goods and Ideas

Native transportation, such as the snowshoe, toboggan, and canoe, were adopted by European adventurers and used by them to map out the interior of North America. The hammock, used by Caribbean peoples, was adopted by sailors as it was comfortable and stored away easily on cramped ships.

Tobacco, used by natives of the Americas in religious rituals, was introduced to Europe by the 1600s. Europeans got addicted to it, and it soon became one of the main export products, helping fuel the economy of the Americas.

Native Adoptions

Native peoples adopted wool to make warm, water-resistant clothing, overcoats, and blankets. They also adopted European metal and iron tools, such as fishhooks, knives, cooking pots, and kettles, to catch, prepare, and cook their food. **Nomadic** people could take along metal items without fear of them breaking, as would earthenware.

Diseases

Europeans unknowingly brought measles, pneumonia, plagues, typhus, chicken pox, and fevers to the native populations. Native peoples hadn't been exposed to these illnesses before. Exposure allows populations to build up some resistance to disease, so without natural **immunity**, the diseases killed entire native communities. Smallpox wiped out one-third to one-half of the native peoples in the Caribbean and in the Aztec and Inca empires.

Sugar

One of the biggest Old World crops to change the New World was sugar cane. Brought to Brazil and the Caribbean, it was used to sweeten bitter drinks such as tea and coffee, which became popular after the Renaissance mainly because they could be sweetened. The sugar cane industry in the Americas brought millions of Africans to the Americas in the centuries after the Renaissance.

Religious Exchange

Religious missionaries, like the Jesuits who came to New France in 1625, brought Catholicism to the indigenous peoples of North America. To teach the basic ideas of Christianity and convert people to the faith, the Jesuits lived among the natives. They described native life in letters, called the *Relations*, which were read widely in Europe.

Before the Spanish brought the horse to America, native peoples, such as the Sioux, Apache, and the Blackfeet, traveled and hunted on foot. With horses they could hunt buffalo over greater distances with greater speed. They became more nomadic and could now carry trade goods, herd animals, and fight in battle, with greater efficiency.

Further Reading and Websites

Wyatt, Valerie. *Who Discovered America?* Toronto: Kids Can Press, 2008
Somervill, Barbara A. *Francisco Pizarro: Conqueror of the Incas.* Compass Point Books, 2005
Owens, Ann-Maureen, and Yealland, Jane. *Kids Book of Canadian Exploration.* Toronto: Kids Can Press, 2004
Doak, Robin S. *Christopher Columbus: Explorer of the New World,* Compass Point Books, 2005

European Explorers www.elizabethan-era.org.uk/european-explorers.htm
The Mariner's Museum: Exploration Through the Ages
   www.mariner.org/exploration/index.php
Hudson River Maritime Museum: Henry Hudson www.hrmm.org/halfmoon/halfmoon.htm
Renaissance Connection www.renaissanceconnection.org
Teacher Oz's Kingdom of History—Renaissance www.teacheroz.com/renaissance.htm
Exhibits Collection—Renaissance www.learner.org/interactives/renaissance

Glossary

allied United or connected

abolition Getting rid of or stopping something

celestial About or relating to the stars and solar system

circumnavigate To sail around the world

commercial Relating to buying and selling, something done for profit

convert Change; to turn someone from one religion to another

criers Men whose job it was to loudly announce or pass on information in public

empire A large group of states or countries under the control of one ruler or government

Hindu Person who believes in Hinduism, a religion; term formerly referring to people from India

immunity Having resistance to disease

missionaries People sent on a mission by a church, often to teach others their religion

Muslim Someone who follows the religion of Islam

navigation Finding a ship's course, position, distance traveled

nomadic Having to do with a lifestyle of wandering in search of food

pelts Skins of furry or wooly animals

pre-existing Something that existed before another; something already there

ultimatum A demand that something be accepted, done, or changed where refusal may result in consequences

Index

Printed in the U.S.A. — CG